METRIC PUZZLES

METRIC PUZZLES

by Peggy Adler and Irving Adler
Illustrated by Peggy Adler

Franklin Watts

New York □ London □ 1977

For Dick

Library of Congress Cataloging in Publication Data

Adler, Peggy.
  Metric puzzles.

  SUMMARY: Puzzles and brain teasers introduce
basic metric vocabulary, symbols, and conversion
tables.
  1. Metric system—Juvenile literature. [1. Metric
system] 1. Adler, Irving, joint author. II. Title.
QC92.5.A34   530'.8   77–1948
ISBN 0–531–01295–6

CONTENTS

BASIC METRIC VOCABULARY, DEFINITIONS, AND SYMBOLS

1 □ WORD SCRAMBLE PUZZLE   Copy or trace each of the sets of squares and circles on this page onto a piece of paper. Unscramble each of the four words below. Then write the letters that spell each word you have unscrambled in the set of squares that goes with that word. Write them in the proper order, putting one letter into each square. Some of the letters will go into squares that have circles inside them. Then these letters will have circles around them.

amrdemi

mrdae

etsmra

geitr

Now put the five circled letters into your copy of the circles below. Put them into the circles in the same order in which they appear in the words that you have unscrambled. Start with the first circled letter in the first word. End with the last circled letter in the fourth word.

The letters that you have put into the circles above spell the name of a unit of length in the metric system. This unit is a little longer than a yard. Its symbol is **m.**

Y	A	R	D	S
M	E	T	E	R

2 □ WORD EVOLUTION PUZZLE   Copy or trace the boxes to the right onto a piece of paper. Change the word YARDS to the word METER. Change one letter at a time. Each time that you change a letter, a correctly spelled word must result for the next line. (There is more than one way to solve this puzzle.)

3 □ WORD SCRAMBLE PUZZLE

erksit

risvle

hemrco

ttare

gatse

ylaro

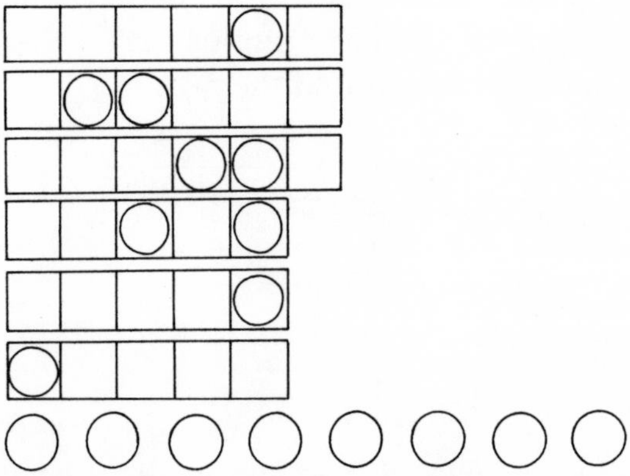

The letters that you have put into the circles above spell the name of another unit of length in the metric system. This unit is one thousand times as long as a meter. It is used in the metric system to measure distances that are measured in miles in the English system. The symbol for this unit is **km**.

4 □ Make as many words as you can from the letters in the word kilometer. (You may not use proper nouns, foreign words, abbreviations, slang, or contractions.)

2

5 □ HIDDEN WORD PUZZLE Hidden in the words that are under the picture is the name of a third unit of length in the metric system. This unit is used to measure lengths that are less than one meter.

My family's move to our new house is recent. I met Erick the first day that we were there. Now he is my best friend.

The unit of length whose name you have found in the hidden word puzzle above is used in the metric system to measure lengths that are measured in inches in the English system. There are one hundred of these small units in one meter. The symbol for this unit is **cm.**

6 ☐ Make as many words as you can from the letters in the word centimeter. (You may not use proper nouns, foreign words, abbreviations, contractions, or slang.)

7 ☐ HIDDEN WORD PUZZLE   Hidden in the words under the picture is the name of a unit of weight in the metric system.

The Great Green Woods are big, rambling, and beautiful. I love to go there for long, leisurely walks.

The unit of weight whose name you have found in the hidden word puzzle above is used in the metric system to measure small weights that are measured in dry ounces or fractions of an ounce in the English system. Its symbol is **g.**

4

8 □ WORD SCRAMBLE PUZZLE

fergfai

talpn

etrme

What metric unit do these letters spell? ◯ ◯ ◯ ◯

9 □ WORD SCRAMBLE PUZZLE

hknit

wsgni

lelvyo

prgea

omrar

◯ ◯ ◯ ◯ ◯ ◯ ◯

The letters that you have put into the circles above spell the name of another unit of weight in the metric system. This unit is one thousand times as heavy as a gram. It is used in the metric system to measure weights that are usually measured in pounds in the English system. The symbol for this unit is **kg.**

5

10 ☐ HIDDEN WORD PUZZLE Hidden in the words under the picture is a word that stands for a unit of volume in the metric system.

When I repaired my car last fall, I terminated all of its rattles and clunks. Now it runs beautifully.

The unit of volume whose name you have found in the hidden word puzzle above is used in the metric system to measure volumes that are usually measured in quarts in the English system. This unit is a little larger than a quart. Its symbol is **l.**

11 □ WORD EVOLUTION PUZZLE   Copy or trace the boxes to the right onto a piece of paper. Change the word PINTS to the word LITER. Change one letter at a time. Each time that you change a letter, a correctly spelled word must result for the next line. (There is more than one way to solve this puzzle.)

P	I	N	T	S
L	I	T	E	R

12 □ HIDDEN WORD PUZZLE   Hidden in the words under the picture is a word that stands for a unit of length in the metric system.

When Tenney goes to sleep at night, she likes to dream eternal dreams.

13 □ METRIC WORD-SEARCH PUZZLE Trace or copy the diagram and letters below onto a piece of paper. The words that are printed to the left of the diagram are hidden in the letters that are inside the diagram. Look for them. The letters of each complete word you are looking for are next to each other in the diagram in the order in which the word is spelled. They may start at the bottom of a row and go up. They may start at the top of a row and go down. Some will be next to each other going from right to left. Others may be next to each other going from left to right. And some, to add to the fun, may be next to each other on a diagonal.

METER
CENTIMETER
KILOMETER
GRAM
KILOGRAM
LITER

L	S	M	A	R	G	L	R	L	N	A	T
I	P	E	P	E	I	N	R	A	R	T	I
T	L	T	C	T	R	E	T	E	M	L	O
E	X	X	E	N	M	C	M	R	A	J	D
Y	G	R	N	C	A	Z	A	J	L	U	A
T	L	Y	T	K	R	R	E	N	E	S	F
P	C	G	I	I	Y	E	R	O	S	P	S
G	C	R	M	L	T	T	Y	A	K	M	L
R	E	A	E	M	I	E	I	I	A	E	U
X	I	S	T	E	C	M	L	A	S	T	S
O	M	T	E	T	E	O	A	F	R	G	K
H	E	V	R	S	G	L	M	E	F	L	I
B	T	O	C	R	N	I	O	O	W	C	L
W	C	L	A	G	G	K	C	L	O	E	O
Q	R	M	R	X	L	B	R	Z	B	N	G
U	A	K	C	I	T	M	S	T	Y	T	X

METRIC UNITS
AND ORDINARY THINGS

14 ☐ Events at track meets are measured in meters. Kurt, Kendra, Erick, and Kim are on Team 8 at the Branford Intermediate School. They are running in an intramural track meet against Team 2. Each child ran in one race in the track meet. The pairs of children ran the following combined distances: Kurt and Kim, 1200 meters (m); Erick and Kim, 1000 m; Kendra and Kim, 900 m; Kurt and Erick, 600 m. How many meters did each of the children run?

15 □ Kurt lives next door to Erick. They live 20 kilometers (km) from the Branford Intermediate School. Every morning, at 7:25 A.M., school bus #5 picks both boys up at the bus stop in front of their homes. After the bus picks up Kurt and Erick, it goes directly to their school, without making any more stops.

One spring morning, when Kurt arrived at the bus stop, Erick was not there. It was such a beautiful day that Erick had decided to ride his bicycle to school. Bus #5, as usual, picked up Kurt at 7:25 A.M. Erick rode his bicycle along the same route that the bus takes to go to the school.

The school bus driver, observing the town speed limit, drove at a steady speed of 40 km per hour. Erick rode his bicycle at his own steady rate of 24 km per hour. What time did Erick have to leave his home on his bicycle in order to arrive at the same time that bus #5 arrived there?

16 □ Kim had a roll of 100 common 13¢ United States postage stamps. She mailed a birthday card to her friend Kendra for 13¢, along with a package of three gift-wrapped trolls, which she sent for 65¢. Kim also mailed her old comic books to her cousins in Idaho for $1.56. If the common United States postage stamp is 2 centimeters (cm) wide, and 2-1/2 cm high, how many centimeters long was Kim's roll of stamps after she had mailed the card, the trolls, and the comic books?

17 □ Tenney is a hedgehog. She would like to know how much she weighs.

1. Tenney and 15 pennies are equal in weight to 93 nickels.

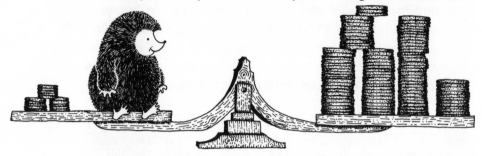

2. Tenney also weighs just as much as 30 pennies and 66 nickels.

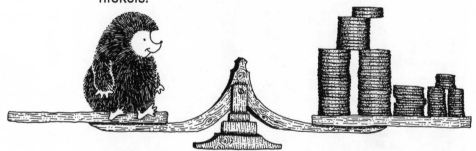

3. One nickel weighs 5 grams (g). Figure out how many nickels weigh just as much as Tenney, and you will know how many grams she weighs.

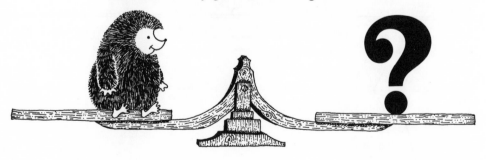

18 □ One day Kendra and Kim went to the meat market. They bought a steak, some hamburger meat, chicken legs, a roast beef, and a turkey. When the butcher weighed the purchases, instead of weighing each purchase separately, he weighed two purchases at a time. First he weighed the steak with each of the other purchases with these results: the steak and the hamburger meat together weighed 5 kilograms (kg); the steak and the chicken legs, 6 kg; the steak and the roast beef, 7 kg; and the steak and the turkey, 9 kg. Then he weighed the hamburger meat and the chicken legs together and found that their combined weight was 7 kg. How many kilograms does each of Kim and Kendra's meat selections weigh?

19 □ Kurt went to the grocery store to buy the refreshments for his school's end-of-the-year picnic. Each one-liter carton of milk cost $1, and each one-liter container of ice cream cost 50¢. Lemonade-mix cost 10¢ for two packets. Each packet of lemonade-mix, mixed with the correct amount of water, makes one liter of lemonade. Kurt bought enough of these items to provide his school with 100 liters of refreshments, at a total cost of $10. How many cartons of milk did he buy? How many containers of ice cream did he buy? How many packets of lemonade-mix did he buy?

CONVERSION PUZZLES

10 meters is about the same as 11 yards.

20 □ Two hedgehogs named Avery and Tenney are sisters. They live 200 meters from the edge of the Great Green Woods. They also live 209 yards from a bubbling stream. Which is closer to their house, the stream or the woods?

21 □ One sunny afternoon Avery was playing among the mushrooms that grow at the edge of the Great Green Woods. She thought that it would be fun to run to the huge rock that lay in the grassy clearing in the middle of the woods. There, in the shadow of the rock, she would take a nap on the cool grass. Avery ran through the woods to the clearing at a speed of 198 yards an hour. When she reached the clearing, she saw that a cat was sleeping on the cool grass in the shadow of the rock. Avery turned around at once in the clearing and ran back on the same path through the Great Green Woods at a rate of 300 meters an hour. She did not stop running until she was out of the woods and was once again among the mushrooms. It took her 29 minutes and 20 seconds to make the entire round trip. How many meters is it from the edge of the Great Green Woods to the clearing?

8 kilometers is about the same as 5 miles.
4 kilometers is about the same as 2-1/2 miles.

22 □ Kendra and Erick are going to have a picnic in a field that is 16 kilometers from where they live. After they eat, they are going to swim in a brook that is 15 miles from where they live. Do they live closer to the field or to the brook?

23 □ Jessica, Vicky, and Tony are three hedgehogs who live in Veblen Grove. They are going to visit their cousins, Tenney and Avery, who live at the edge of the Great Green Woods. At a point 120 miles from the Great Green Woods, Jessica, Vicky, and Tony passed Tenney and Avery. Tenney and Avery were on their way to Veblen Grove to visit Jessica, Vicky, and Tony. The two groups of hedgehogs did not see each other as they passed each other, because Tenney and Avery were going

through a hollow log that lay in the middle of the path at the same time that Jessica, Vicky, and Tony were walking across the top of it.

When Tenney and Avery arrived at Jessica, Vicky, and Tony's home in Veblen Grove, they found a note on the door that said, "Have gone to visit our cousins who live near the edge of the Great Green Woods. Will be back when we get back." So, Tenney and Avery turned around and started to go back to their own home near the Great Green Woods. At a point 256 kilometers from Veblen Grove Tenney and Avery met Jessica, Vicky, and Tony. Their three cousins had reached their home near the Great Green Woods, where they had found a note on the door. The note had said, "Gone to Veblen Grove. Will be back when you see us again." And so, Jessica, Vicky, and Tony had turned around and were on their way back to their own home in Veblen Grove when the five cousins met. Each group of hedgehogs moved at its own steady pace both ways. Can you figure out how many kilometers the Great Green Woods are from Veblen Grove?

17

5 centimeters is about the same as 2 inches.
2-1/2 centimeters is about the same as 1 inch.

24 □ Tenney's bed is one foot long. Avery's bed is 32-1/2 centimeters long. Which hedgehog has the longer bed?

25 □ Tenney is pulling Avery on a sled that is 35 centimeters long. They are going to cross a path which is 35 cm wide. Tenney is pulling the sled at the rate of 10 feet a minute. If she pulls the sled straight across the path, how long will it take for it to cross the path?

28 grams is about the same as 1 ounce.

26 □ Tony and Vicky are picking mushrooms. If Tony picks 10 ounces of mushrooms and Vicky picks 336 grams of mushrooms, which hedgehog will pick the heavier crop of mushrooms?

18

27 □ Avery is making tea. Her new box of 100 tea bags weighs 8 ounces. This week, Avery will have one cup of tea for breakfast on each of the following days: Monday, Tuesday, Friday, and Sunday. On Wednesday, Thursday, and Saturday, she will have two cups of tea for breakfast. During the same week, Avery will also have a cup of tea in the mid-afternoon every day except Sunday. Avery uses a new tea bag for each cup of tea that she makes. At the end of one week, how many grams will the tea bags that are left in the box weigh?

10 kilograms is about the same as 22 pounds.
5 kilograms is about the same as 11 pounds.

28 ☐ When Kendra's puppy reaches its adult size, it will weigh 77 pounds. When Kurt's puppy reaches its adult size, it will weigh 20 kilograms. Which child's puppy will weigh more when each of the two puppies has reached its adult size?

29 □ Erick has a pile of books that weighs 5 kilograms. Each of Erick's books weighs one pound. He wants to give them to his friends Kurt, Kim, and Kendra.

Because Kurt is the oldest of the three children, Erick wants to give him one-half of the books. Because Kim is only a little bit younger than Kurt, Erick wants to give her one-fourth of the books. And Since Kendra is the youngest, Erick wants to give her one-sixth of the books.

When Erick was ready to give each of the three children their books, he realized that he could not give them their books without tearing some of them up. Since owning torn books is worse than owning no books at all, Erick asked the other children what he should do. Kim, who is good in arithmetic, said that she knew how to solve the problem. She went to her own house, and when she returned, she showed Erick how to divide the books without having to tear any of them. How many books did each child get?

1 liter is slightly larger than 1 quart.

For conversions involving small numbers of quarts or liters, use this rule:

1 liter is about the same as 1 quart.

For conversions involving large numbers of quarts or liters, use this rule:

19 liters is about the same as 20 quarts or 5 gallons.

30 □ Kim drinks 2 gallons of milk a week. Kendra drinks 6 liters of milk a week. Which of the two girls drinks more milk in one week?

31 □ Kurt and Erick went to Peddler's Drive Farm to buy some milk. Kurt carried a 5-liter can and Erick carried a 4-liter can. The woman who owned the farm had two cans filled with milk. There were 10-1/2 gallons of milk in each can. Each boy wanted her to pour 2 liters of milk into his own can. Using only the four cans, how did she measure the milk for Kurt and Erick?

METRIC PREFIXES

Sometimes, when you are measuring something, the basic metric units—the meter, the gram, or the liter—may be too big to use. Sometimes they may be too small to use. When this happens you must then use larger or smaller metric units. Each of these larger or smaller metric units is named by putting a prefix in front of the name of the basic metric unit from which you are getting the larger or smaller unit. The same metric prefixes are used in front of the names of all of the different basic metric units.

SMALLER UNITS

If you want to measure a length that is smaller than a meter, a unit that is smaller than a meter is needed. One kind of smaller unit is obtained by dividing a meter into ten equal pieces. Each of these pieces is a new unit, and is called a *decimeter.* Its symbol is **dm.** There are 10 decimeters in one meter. If these units turn out to be too long, you can get another smaller unit by dividing the decimeter into ten equal pieces. Each of these pieces is called a *centimeter.* Its symbol is **cm.** There are 10 centimeters in one decimeter, and 100 centimeters in one meter. To get smaller and smaller units, continue the process of obtaining smaller units by dividing by 10. The next smaller unit after the centimeter is the *millimeter*. Its symbol is **mm**. There are 10 millimeters in one centimeter. There are 100 millimeters in one decimeter. And there are 1000 millimeters in one meter. Each of the smaller units is a fraction of one meter, and the prefix used in the name of the unit identifies the fraction.

Deci means one-tenth. One decimeter = one-tenth of a meter = 1/10 of a meter = 0.1 meter. Centi means one-hundredth. One centimeter = one-hundredth of a meter = 1/100 of a meter = 0.01 meter. Milli means one-thousandth. One millimeter = one-thousandth of a meter = 1/1000 of a meter = 0.001 meter. One millimeter is one-tenth of a centimeter, so 1 mm = 0.1 cm.

10 decimeters = 1 meter;	10 dm = 1 m.
100 centimeters = 1 meter;	100 cm = 1 m.
1000 millimeters = 1 meter;	1000 mm = 1 m.
10 millimeters = 1 centimeter;	10 mm = 1 cm.

The division of a meter into decimeters and centimeters is like the division of a dollar into dimes and cents:

10 decimeters = 1 meter, just as 10 dimes = 1 dollar;
100 centimeters = 1 meter, just as 100 cents = 1 dollar;
10 centimeters = 1 decimeter, just as 10 cents = 1 dime.

The prefix *milli* that occurs in the name *milli*meter also occurs in the name *milli*gram. It has the same meaning in both places, namely, "one thousandth of."

1 millimeter = one thousandth of a meter = 0.001 m.
1 milligram = one thousandth of a gram = 0.001 g.

LARGER UNITS

If you want to measure a length that is very much larger than a meter, a unit that is larger than a meter may be useful. One kind of larger unit is obtained by multiplying the meter by 10. This new unit that is 10 meters long is called a *decameter.* There are 10 meters in one decameter. If this unit turns out to be too small, you can get another, larger unit, by multiplying the decameter by 10. This new unit is 100 meters long and is called a *hectometer.* There are 10 decameters in one hectometer, and 100 meters in one hectometer. To get larger and larger units, continue the process of obtaining larger units by multiplying by 10. The next larger unit after the hectometer is the kilometer. There are 10 hectometers in one kilometer. There are 100 decameters in one kilometer. And there are 1000 meters in one kilometer. Each of the larger units is a multiple of one meter, and the prefix used in the name of the unit identifies the multiple.

Deca means ten times. One decameter = ten times one meter = 10×1 meter = 10 meters. Hecto means one hundred times. One hectometer = one hundred times one meter = 100×1 meter = 100 meters. Kilo means one thousand times. One kilometer = one thousand times one meter = 1000×1 meter = 1000 meters.

$$1 \text{ decameter} = 10 \text{ meters}$$
$$1 \text{ hectometer} = 100 \text{ meters}$$
$$1 \text{ kilometer} = 1000 \text{ meters}$$

The prefix *kilo* that occurs in the name *kilo*meter also occurs in the name *kilo*gram. It has the same meaning in both places, namely, "one thousand times."

$$1 \text{ kilometer} = \text{one thousand times one meter} = 1000 \text{ meters.}$$
$$1 \text{ kilogram} = \text{one thousand times one gram} = 1000 \text{ grams.}$$

THE ADVANTAGE OF GROUPING BY TENS

The system of Arabic numerals, which is our way of writing numbers, uses grouping by tens:

ten units   = 1 ten   = 10
ten tens   = 1 hundred   = 100
ten hundreds = 1 thousand = 1000

The metric system also uses grouping by tens. So the grouping in the metric system matches the grouping in the way we write numbers. This is a great advantage, because it makes the arithmetic of changing units very easy. The arithmetic of changing metric units is explained in the next section.

The English system of measures does not have this advantage because it does grouping by numbers like 3, 12, and 16 that are different from 10. For example, 3 feet = 1 yard; 12 inches = 1 foot; 16 ounces = 1 pound.

THE ARITHMETIC OF CHANGING FROM ONE METRIC UNIT TO ANOTHER

A change from one metric unit to another involves multiplying by either 10 or 0.1 one or more times. The multiplication can be carried out simply by moving the decimal point according to three rules:

1. In a whole number the decimal point is understood to be immediately to the right of the units digit. Thus, 12 and 12. mean the same thing.
2. To multiply a number by 10, move the decimal point one place to the right. For example, to calculate 10 × 2.3, move the decimal point in 2.3 one place to the right as shown by the curved arrow: 10 × 2.3 = 23.

3. To multiply a number by 0.1, or one-tenth, move the decimal point one place to the left. For example, to calculate 0.1×2.3, move the decimal point in 2.3 one place to the left as shown by the curved arrow: $0.1 \times 2.3 = .23$.

EXAMPLE   Change 2 meters to centimeters.

$$
\begin{aligned}
2 \text{ meters} &= 2 \times (1 \text{ meter}) \\
&= 2 \times (100 \text{ centimeters}) \\
&= (2 \times 100) \text{ centimeters} \\
&= (100 \times 2.) \text{ centimeters} \\
&= (10 \times 10 \times 2.) \text{ centimeters} \\
&= (10 \times 20.) \text{ centimeters} \\
&= 200. \text{ centimeters}
\end{aligned}
$$

Notice that each multiplication by 10 moves the decimal point one place to the right. Multiplication by 10×10 moves the decimal point two places to the right.

EXAMPLE   Change 5 millimeters to centimeters.

$$
\begin{aligned}
5 \text{ millimeters} &= 5 \times (1 \text{ millimeter}) \\
&= 5 \times (\text{one-tenth of a centimeter}) \\
&= 5 \times (0.1 \text{ centimeter}) \\
&= (5 \times 0.1) \text{ centimeter} \\
&= (0.1 \times 5.) \text{ centimeter} \\
&= 0.5 \text{ centimeter}
\end{aligned}
$$

Notice that multiplication by 0.1 moves the decimal point in 5. one place to the left.

32 □ Two cookbooks sat side by side on a shelf in Erick's

kitchen. One day a hungry bookworm began at page one of the first cookbook (the one on the left) and ate its way to the last page of the second cookbook (the one on the right). The cover of each of the two cookbooks is 3 millimeters thick. Each cookbook, without its covers, is 5 centimeters thick. How many centimeters did the bookworm travel?

33 □ Every morning when Kendra has her breakfast, she takes one orange-flavored Vitamin C tablet. She takes a 250 milligram (mg) tablet every day from Halloween through April Fools' Day, inclusive. All of the other days of the year Kendra takes a 100 mg tablet with her breakfast. How many grams of Vitamin C does Kendra take in one leap year?

34 ☐ Kim went to the store to buy some odds and ends. With her she brought her owl bank, which was filled with pennies. All of the pennies in Kim's bank, together, weighed 3 hectograms (hg).

Kim bought some velvet ribbons for her hair for 15 decagrams (dkg) of pennies. She spent 75 grams of pennies to buy some colored pencils. She bought a crossword puzzle magazine for 6 decagrams of pennies, and a pack of sugarless gum with her last 15 grams of pennies.

If one penny weighs 3 grams, how much money did Kim bring to the store? How much money did each of Kim's purchases cost?

35 □ This baby mountain lion is having her breakfast. The baby bottle from which she is drinking holds 120 milliliters (ml) of milk. If she drinks milk from the same size bottle three times a day, how many liters of milk will she drink in one week?

AREA

Area measurements are usually made in square units. When you want to measure the area of a square or of a rectangle, you divide that area into unit squares, each of which is one unit long and one unit wide. You then count these unit squares. Thus, if you want to measure the area of a rectangle that is 5 units long, and 4 units wide, you will divide the rectangle into unit squares and count them. In this case, you will count

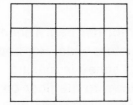

20 unit squares. Therefore, the area of the rectangle is 20 square units.

There is also a faster way to find the area of the same rectangle. There are 5 rows of unit squares in the rectangle. There are 4 unit squares in each of these 5 rows. Therefore, the number of unit squares in the rectangle is equal to 4×5 unit squares = 20 unit squares = 20 square units. In general, for a square or for a rectangle, area = length $\times$ width.

In the English system, the units that are used to measure length are inches, feet, yards, and miles. Therefore, areas in the English system are expressed in square inches, square feet, square yards, and square miles. Land measures in the English system are also expressed in acres.

In the metric system, the most common metric units that are used to measure length are meters, centimeters, and kilometers. Therefore, the most common square units in the metric system are square meters, square centimeters, and square kilometers.

The metric units used to measure land area are the *are* and the *hectare.* One are is 10 meters long by 10 meters wide, or 10 m × 10 m = 100 square meters. One hectare is 100 m × 100 m = 10,000 square meters. One hundred ares = one hectare. Ten thousand ares = one hundred hectares = one square kilometer.

36 □ What is the area of the common United States postage stamp? (See puzzle 16.)

37 □ Tenney is making a patchwork quilt for her bed. Tenney's bed is 30 centimeters long and 20 centimeters wide. Her bed is also 10 centimeters high. The quilt that Tenney is making will cover her entire bed. It will also come down to the floor on all four of the bed's sides. What will be the area of her quilt in square meters?

VOLUME

Volume measurements are usually made in cubic units. When you want to measure the volume of a cube or of a rectangular box you divide it into unit cubes each of which is one unit long, one unit wide, and one unit high. You then count the unit cubes. The number of unit cubes that you will count will tell you the volume. Thus, if you divide into unit cubes a rectangular box that is 5 units long, 4 units wide, and 3 units high, you will count 60 unit cubes. Therefore, the volume of the rectangular box is

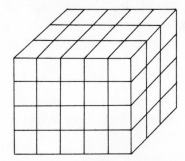

60 cubic units. There is also a faster way to find the volume of the same rectangular box. There are three layers of unit cubes in the rectangular box. Each of the three layers of unit cubes contains four rows of unit cubes. There are also five unit cubes in each of these four rows. Therefore, the number of unit cubes in the rectangular box is equal to $3 \times 4 \times 5 = 60$. You are multiplying the number of units in the length of the rec-

tangular box by the number of units in its width, and by the number of units in its height, to get the number of cubic units in its volume. Thus, for a cube or for a rectangular box, volume = length × width × height.

In the English system, some of the cubic units that are used are the cubic inch, the cubic foot, and the cubic yard. Teaspoons, tablespoons, fluid ounces, cups, pints, quarts, gallons, and bushels are also units of volume in the English system, but they are not called cubic units.

Some of the cubic units in the metric system are cubic millimeters (cmm), cubic centimeters (cc), and cubic meters (cu m). Other units of volume in the metric system are the liter and the milliliter.

A liter is the volume of a cube that is 10 centimeters long, 10 centimeters wide, and 10 centimeters high, or 10 cm × 10 cm × 10 cm = 1000 cubic centimeters. Therefore, one liter is the same as 1000 cubic centimeters. One liter is also equal to one thousand milliliters. Therefore, one milliliter = one cubic centimeter. One cubic meter is equal to one thousand liters. One teaspoon = 5 cubic centimeters, and one tablespoon = 15 cubic centimeters.

38 □ A one-quarter pound bar of margarine is 3 centimeters wide, 3 centimeters high, and 12 centimeters long. What is the volume of the bar of margarine?

39 □ A recipe for a French omelet calls for the use of one tablespoon of cooking oil to fry one omelet made with three eggs. How many such omelets can be made with one liter of cooking oil?

TEMPERATURE

Temperature is measured in units called degrees. In the English system, temperature is measured in degrees Fahrenheit. The symbol for degree is °. The symbol for Fahrenheit is F. In the English system, the temperature at sea level at which water boils is 212° F. The temperature at sea level at which water freezes is 32° F.

In the metric system, temperature is measured in degrees Celsius. The symbol for degrees is still °. The symbol for Celsius is C. In the metric system, the temperature at sea level at which water boils, is 100° C. The temperature at sea level at which water freezes is 0° C. Therefore, 0° C = 32° F, and 100° C = 212° F. Temperatures that are below 0° C are expressed in minus degrees. Thus, five degrees below 0° C is written as –5° C.

To convert from degrees Fahrenheit to degrees Celsius, you subtract 32° from the number of degrees that it is Fahrenheit, and then you multiply by 5/9. Therefore, to change from 68° F to degrees Celsius, you subtract 32° from 68°, and then multiply by 5/9. 68° – 32° = 36°; 5/9 × 36° = 20°. Therefore, 68° F is the same as 20° C.

To change from degrees Celsius to degrees Fahrenheit, you multiply the number of degrees that it is Celsius by 9/5, and then you add 32°. Therefore, to change from 70° C to degrees Fahrenheit, you multiply 70° by 9/5, and then you add 32°. 9/5 × 70° = 126°. 126° + 32° = 158°. Therefore, 70° C is the same as 158° F.

40 □ The temperature today is 30° C. If Erick's home is at sea level, will he be able to go sledding on the hill near his house?

MORE METRIC PUZZLES...
TO TEST YOUR
METRIC UNDERSTANDING

41 □ One sunny summer morning Kim went fishing at Stony Creek. At the end of the day she returned home, bringing with her the one fish that she had caught. Kim called Kendra and invited her to come to her house that night for a fish feast. Kendra asked Kim, "How much did the fish that you caught weigh?" Kim replied, "The tail weighs 250 grams. The weight of the head is equal to the weight of the tail plus one half of the weight of the body. The weight of the body is equal in weight to the weight of the head plus the weight of the tail." How many kilograms did Kim's fish weigh?

42 □ An air plant doubles its weight every 30 seconds. After twenty minutes it weighs one kilogram. When will it weigh 1/2 kilogram? When will it weigh 500 grams?

43 □ Kurt and Erick took a bus from their home town of Branford, to Sleeping Giant Park in Mt. Carmel. The two boys only had enough money between them to ride one way. Therefore, they had to walk back home. The bus traveled at a speed of 60 kilometers per hour. Kurt and Erick walked at a rate of 20 kilometers per hour. The boys began their walk home, along the same route that the bus had driven, as soon as they got off the bus. If the entire round trip took 8 hours, how far is Sleeping Giant Park from Branford?

44 □ The town of Crosswood has 45 miles of streets to plow after a snowstorm. Nine snowplows are used to clear the streets. Therefore, each snowplow clears an average of how many kilometers of street?

45 □ Two bicyclists start traveling toward each other at the same time from two towns that are 400 kilometers apart. One of the cyclists is traveling at the speed of 16 kilometers per hour. The other cyclist is traveling at the speed of 24 kilometers per hour. At the very same moment that the two cyclists start their journey, a fly named Walden, who was perched on the front wheel of the slower bicycle, leaves the front wheel of that bicycle, and, flying at a speed of 32 kilometers per hour, heads toward the other bicycle. As soon as he reaches the other bicycle, he touches its front wheel, turns right around, and flies back toward the first bicycle. As the two bicyclists approach each other, Walden continues flying back and forth, touching the front wheel of each of the two bicycles, in turn, until, alas, the bicycles crash, and he is crushed between their two front wheels. How many trips back and forth did Walden make before he met with his tragic end? How many kilometers did he travel altogether?

46 □ Every morning, Erick sprinkles 2 teaspoons of sugar into his breakfast cereal, Kurt sprinkles 5 cubic centimeters (cc) of sugar into his cereal, and Kim sprinkles 10 milliliters of sugar into her cereal. Which child's cereal has the most sugar sprinkled into it?

47 □ A newspaper reporting the birth of a normal, full-term baby gave its birth-weight as 3, without mentioning the unit of weight being used. What is the omitted unit likely to be?

48 □ Peddler's Drive Farm has an area of 50 hectares. What is the area of Peddler's Drive Farm in square meters?

49 □ How many millimeters are there in half a centimeter?

50 □ Which distance is longer, 30 meters or 32 yards?

51 □ Match each prefix with its meaning:

milli	ten times
centi	one thousand times
deca	one-hundredth of
kilo	one-thousandth of

52 □ Kendra and Kim started walking around a circular track at the same time. Kendra walked at a speed of 75 meters per minute, and Kim walked at a speed of 65 meters per minute. If the next time that they were together again was one hour and twenty minutes after they had started, how many miles long is the track?

ANSWERS AND EXPLANATIONS

1□ m e r (m) a i d
    d r (e) a m
    s (t) r (e) a m   =   (m)(e)(t)(e)(r)
    t i g e (r)

2□ Y A R D S
    Y A R N S
    D A R N S
    D A R E S
    M A R E S
    M A T E S
    M A T E R
    M E T E R

3□ s t r i (k) e
    s (i)(l) v e r
    c h r (o)(m) e
    t r (e) a (t)   =   (k)(i)(l)(o)(m)(e)(t)(e)(r)
    s t a g (e)
    (r) o y a l

4□ Some of the words that you can make from the letters in the word kilometer are: ire, irk, it, kit, kite, let, like, lime, me, meet, met, meter, milk, mole, more, oil, rite, tile, time, timer, tire, toil, tore, and tree.

39

5 □ centimeter

6 □ Some of the words that you can make from the letters in the word centimeter are: cent, center, enter, entire, ice, in, ire, it, me, meet, men, mere, met, meter, mice, mine, miner, mite, nice, nicer, recent, remit, rent, ten, tent, term, time, timer, tire, and trite.

7 □ gram

8 □ (g) i (r) a f f e
     p l (a) n t   =   (g)(r)(a)(m)
     (m) e t e r

9 □ t h i n (k)
     s w (i) n g
     (l)(o) v e l y   =   (k)(i)(l)(o)(g)(r)(a)(m)
     (g)(r) a p e
     (a) r (m) o r

10 □ liter

11 □ P I N T S
      L I N T S
      L I N E S
      L I N E R
      L I T E R

12 □ meter

40

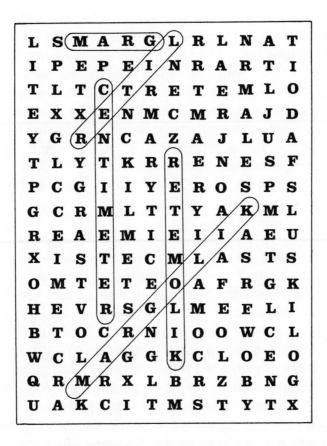

```
L S M A R G L R L N A T
I P E P E I N R A R T I
T L T C T R E T E M L O
E X X E N M C M R A J D
Y G R N C A Z A J L U A
T L Y T K R R E N E S F
P C G I I Y E R O S P S
G C R M L T T Y A K M L
R E A E M I E I I A E U
X I S T E C M L A S T S
O M T E T E O A F R G K
H E V R S G L M E F L I
B T O C R N I O O W C L
W C L A G G K C L O E O
Q R M R X L B R Z B N G
U A K C I T M S T Y T X
```

14 □ Since Kurt and Kim ran 1200 meters together, and Erick and Kim ran 1000 m together, Kurt ran 200 m more than Erick. But Kurt's distance plus Erick's distance is 600 m. Then 200 m plus twice Erick's distance is 600 m. This means that twice Erick's distance is 400 m, and Erick's distance is 200 m. Since Erick and Kim ran 1000 m altogether, Kim's distance = 1000 m − 200 m = 800 m. Since Kurt and Kim together ran 1200 m, Kurt's distance = 1200 m − 800 m = 400 m. Since Kendra and Kim ran 900 m altogether, Kendra's distance = 900 m − 800 m = 100 m.

15 □ Bus #5 drove the 20 kilometers to the school at a speed of 40 kilometers per hour (kmph). Therefore, the length of time that that it took for the bus to reach the school was 20 km ÷ 40 kmph = 1/2 hour. Since one-half hour is the same as thirty minutes, bus #5 arrived at the school at 7:25 A.M. + 30 minutes = 7:55 A.M. Erick rode the same 20 km at the rate of 24 kmph. Thus, the length of time that it took for Erick to ride his bicycle from his home to the school was 20 km ÷ 24 kmph = 5/6 of an hour = 50 minutes. Now subtract 50 minutes from 7:55 A.M. and you will know what time Erick left for school. 7:55 A.M. − 50 minutes = 7:05 A.M.

16 □ Kim mailed the card for 13¢. Therefore she used one stamp to send the card. The cost of the postage for the three gift-wrapped trolls was 65¢. Since each stamp costs 13¢, the number of stamps Kim had to use to mail the trolls = 65¢ ÷ 13¢ = 5. The postage for the comic books was $1.56. So the number of stamps used to mail the comic books = $1.56 ÷ 13¢ = 12.

Now add together the total number of 13¢ stamps that Kim used to mail the card, the trolls, and the comic books. One stamp + 5 stamps + 12 stamps = 18 stamps. Now we know that Kim used 18 of the stamps from the roll. She started with a roll of 100 stamps, and 100 stamps − 18 stamps = 82 stamps. Therefore, Kim had 82 stamps left on the roll. We already know that one common United States postage stamp is 2 centimeters wide. Therefore, a roll of 82 such stamps is 82 × 2 cm, or 164 centimeters long.

17 □ Add 15 pennies to each side of the scale in picture 2. Both sides will still balance, because you have added the same number of pennies to each side, and all of the pennies are equal in

weight. Now the left side of the scale in picture 2 is the same as the left side of the scale in picture 1.

In the first picture, Tenney and 15 pennies = 93 nickels. In the second picture, after the 15 pennies have been added, Tenney and 15 pennies = 66 nickels and 45 pennies. Now you can say that 93 nickels weigh the same as 45 pennies and 66 nickels. Therefore, 45 pennies weigh just as much as 27 nickels. And since 45 and 27 can both be divided by 9, then every 5 pennies weigh just as much as every 3 nickels. Thus, 30 pennies are equal in weight to 18 nickels. Then you can replace the 30 pennies on the right side of picture 2 by 18 nickels. Eighteen nickels + 66 nickels = 84 nickels. Therefore, 84 nickels weigh just the same as Tenney. And, because one nickel weighs 5 grams (g), Tenney then weighs 84×5 g, or 420 g.

18 □ Since the steak and the hamburger meat together weigh 5 kilograms (kg), while the steak and the chicken legs together weigh 6 kg, the chicken legs weigh 1 kg more than the hamburger meat. Since the hamburger meat and the chicken legs together weigh 7 kg, that means that twice the weight of the hamburger meat plus 1 kg = 7 kg. Then twice the weight of the hamburger meat is 6 kg, and the hamburger meat weighs 3 kg. Then the chicken legs weigh 7 kg – 3 kg = 4 kg. Then the steak weighs 5 kg – 3 kg = 6 kg – 4 kg = 2 kg. Since the steak and the roast beef together weigh 7 kg, the roast beef weighs 7 kg – 2 kg = 5 kg. Since the steak and the turkey together weigh 9 kg, the turkey weighs 9 kg – 2 kg = 7 kg.

19 □ Kurt bought one liter of milk for $1, 9 liters of ice cream for $4.50, and 90 packets of lemonade-mix costing $4.50, which when mixed with water, yield 90 liters of lemonade.

20 □ For a quick estimate, to change from meters to yards, replace every 10 meters by 11 yards. Since 200 m ÷ 10 m = 20, 200 m = 20 × (10 m) = about 20 × (11 yd) = about 220 yards. Therefore, Tenney and Avery live 220 yards from the edge of the Great Green Woods. Since the bubbling stream is 209 yards from their house, they live 11 yards closer to the stream than they do to the woods. Notice that you divide the number of meters by 10 meters to find out how many times 10 meters it is. Then you write 11 yards in the place of 10 meters.

For a quick estimate, to change from yards to meters, replace every 11 yards by 10 meters. Since 209 yd ÷ 11 yd = 19, 209 yd = 19 × (11 yd) = about 19 × (10 m) = about 190 meters. Therefore, Tenney and Avery live 190 meters from the bubbling stream. Since the Great Green Woods is 200 meters from their home, they live 10 meters closer to the stream than they do to the woods. Notice that you divide the number of yards by 11 yards to find out how many times 11 yards it is. Then you write 10 meters in the place of 11 yards.

21 □ First convert yards to meters: 198 yd = 18 × (11 yd) = about 18 × (10 m) = about 180 m. So, Avery ran from the edge of the woods to the clearing at a speed of 180 meters per hour. Therefore, she ran one meter toward the clearing in 20 seconds. She ran one meter away from the clearing in 12 seconds. So each meter that Avery ran through the woods, to and from the clearing, took her 32 seconds. The whole trip took her 29 minutes and 20 seconds, or 1760 seconds. Now divide 1760 seconds by 32 seconds to find the number of meters from the edge of the Great Green Woods to the clearing. The distance from the edge of the woods to the clearing is 55 meters.

22 □ For a quick estimate, to change from kilometers to miles,

replace every 8 kilometers by 5 miles. Since 16 km ÷ 8 km = 2, 16 km = 2 × (8 km) = about 2 × (5 mi) = about 10 mi. Therefore, Kendra and Erick live 10 miles from the field. Since the brook is 15 miles from where they live, they live 5 miles closer to the field than they do to the brook. Notice that you divide the number of kilometers by 8 kilometers to find out how many times 8 kilometers it is. Then you write 5 miles in the place of 8 kilometers.

For a quick estimate, to change from miles to kilometers, replace every 5 miles by 8 kilometers. Since 15 mi ÷ 5 mi = 3, 15 mi = 3 × (5 mi) = about 3 × (8 km) = about 24 km. Therefore, Kendra and Erick live 24 kilometers from the brook. Since the field is 16 kilometers from where they live, they live 8 kilometers closer to the field than they do to the brook. Notice that you divide the number of miles by 5 miles to find out how many times 5 miles it is. Then you write 8 kilometers in the place of 5 miles.

23 ☐ The distance between the Great Green Woods and Veblen Grove is 320 kilometers.

When the five hedgehogs passed each other, on the way to visit each other, Tenney and Avery had gone 120 miles from the Great Green Woods. The distance that Tenney and Avery had gone, plus the distance that Jessica, Vicky, and Tony had gone, equals the distance between the two towns.

When Tenney and Avery and their cousins met, on the way back to their own homes, the distance that Jessica, Vicky, and Tony had gone, plus the distance that Tenney and Avery had gone, was equal to three times the distance between Veblen Grove and the Great Green Woods. Then since each group of hedgehogs moved at a steady pace, the distance that each of the two groups traveled until they met is three times the distance that it had traveled when they had first passed each other.

Tenney and Avery were 120 miles from the Great Green Woods when they passed Jessica, Vicky, and Tony. Since 8 kilometers is about the same as 5 miles, for a quick estimate, to change from miles to kilometers, replace every 5 miles by 8 kilometers. Since 120 mi ÷ 5 mi = 24, 120 mi = 24 × (5 mi) = about 24 × (8 km) = about 192 km.

When Tenney and Avery met Jessica, Vicky, and Tony on their way back home, they had walked three times as far, or 576 kilometers. This distance of 576 kilometers consists of two parts, the full distance from the Great Green Woods to Veblen Grove, plus the 256 kilometers back to the point where the cousins met. Therefore the distance between the Great Green Woods and Veblen Grove is 576 km − 256 km = 320 km.

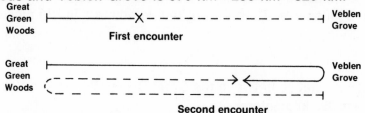

24 □ For a quick estimate, to change from inches to centimeters, replace every 2 inches by 5 centimeters. Since one foot is the same as 12 inches, and 12 in ÷ 2 in = 6, 12 in = 6 × (2 in) = about 6 × (5 cm) = about 30 cm. Therefore, Tenney's bed is 30 centimeters long. Since Avery's bed is 32-1/2 centimeters long, her bed is 2-1/2 centimeters longer than Tenney's bed. Notice that you divide the number of inches by 2 inches to find out how many times 2 inches it is. Then you write 5 centimeters in the place of 2 inches.

For a quick estimate, to change from centimeters to inches, replace every 2-1/2 centimeters by one inch. Since 32-1/2 cm ÷ 2-1/2 cm = 13, 32-1/2 cm = 13 × (2-1/2 cm) = about 13 × (1 in) =

about 13 in. Therefore, Avery's bed is 13 inches long. Since Avery's bed is 13 inches long, her bed is one inch longer than Tenney's bed. Notice that you divide the number of centimeters by 2-1/2 cm to find out how many times 2-1/2 cm it is. Then you write one inch in the place of 2-1/2 cm.

25 □ When the sled starts to cross the path, the front end of the sled will touch one side of the path, but all of the sled will be off the path. After the sled has moved 35 centimeters, the front end of it will touch the other side of the path, and all of the sled will be on the path. After the sled has moved another 35 centimeters, the rear end of it will have just left the path. So the time that it will take for the sled to cross the path is the same as the time that it will take for the sled to move 70 centimeters. Tenney is pulling the sled at the rate of 10 feet a minute. Ten feet = 10×12 in = 120 in. And 120 in = $60 \times (2$ in) = about $60 \times (5$ cm) = about 300 cm. So the sled moves 300 centimeters per minute, or 5 centimeters per second. Since $70 \div 5 = 14$, the sled moves 70 centimeters in 14 seconds. Then it takes 14 seconds for Tenney to pull the sled across the path.

26 □ For a quick estimate, to change from grams to ounces, replace every 28 grams by one ounce. Since 336 g ÷ 28 g = 12, 336 g = $12 \times (28$ g) = about $12 \times (1$ oz) = about 12 oz. Therefore, Vicky picked 12 ounces of mushrooms. Since Tony picked 10 ounces of mushrooms, the crop that Vicky picked is 2 ounces heavier.

For a quick estimate, to change from ounces to grams, replace every one ounce by 28 grams. Since 10 oz ÷ 1 oz = 10, 10 oz = $10 \times (1$ oz) = about $10 \times (28$ g) = about 28 g. Therefore, Tony picked 280 grams of mushrooms. Since Vicky picked 336 grams of mushrooms, the crop that she picked is 56 grams heavier.

27 □ Avery had one cup of tea for breakfast on Monday, Tuesday, Friday, and Sunday, or 4 cups of tea in all. On Wednesday, Thursday, and Saturday, she had two cups of tea for breakfast, or 6 cups of tea in all. We also know that Avery had one cup of tea every day except Sunday in the mid-afternoon during that same week. Avery had 6 mid-afternoon cups of tea. So, at the end of one week, Avery had a total of 4 cups + 6 cups + 6 cups = 16 cups of tea. And since she used a new tea bag for each cup of tea that she made, she used a total of 16 tea bags in one week.

Avery's new box of 100 tea bags weighs 8 ounces. Eight ounces = $8 \times (1 \text{ oz})$ = about $8 \times (28 \text{ g})$ = about 224 g. So, the total weight of the 100 tea bags in the box is 224 grams. To find out how many grams each of the 100 tea bags weighs, you divide 224 grams by 100. Each tea bag weighs about 2-1/4 grams. Since Avery used 16 tea bags, 84 tea bags were left in the box at the end of the week. They weigh about $84 \times 2\text{-}1/4 \text{ g}$ = 189 g.

28 □ For a quick estimate, to change from kilograms to pounds, replace every 10 kilograms by 22 pounds. Since 20 kg ÷ 10 kg = 2, 20 kg = $2 \times (10 \text{ kg})$ = about $2 \times (22 \text{ lb})$ = about 44 lbs. Therefore, when Kurt's puppy reaches its adult size, it will weigh 44 pounds. Since Kendra's puppy will weigh 77 pounds when it reaches its adult size, her fully grown dog will weigh 33 pounds more than Kurt's.

For a quick estimate, to change from pounds to kilograms, replace every 11 pounds by 5 kilograms. Since 77 lb ÷ 11 lb = 7, 77 lb = $7 \times (11 \text{ lb})$ = about $7 \times (5 \text{ kg})$ = about 35 kg. Therefore, when Kendra's puppy reaches its adult size it will weigh 35 kilograms. Since Kurt's puppy will weigh 20 kilograms when it reaches its adult size, Kendra's fully grown dog will weigh 15 kilograms more than Kurt's.

29 □ Erick's pile of books weighs 5 kilograms, or about 11 pounds. Since each one of his books weighs one pound, he therefore has a total of 11 books to divide among his friends.

Kim brought back one of her own books from her own house. She added it to Erick's 11 books. Now there were 12 books. She then gave Kurt 6 of Erick's books, since one-half of 12 is 6. She herself took 3 of Erick's books, since one-fourth of 12 is 3. Kim then gave Kendra 2 of Erick's books, since one-sixth of 12 is 2. 6 books + 3 books + 2 books = 11 books. The book that Kim had brought from her own house was left over, and so she took it back home with her.

30 □ For a quick estimate, to change from liters to quarts, replace every one liter by one quart. 6 l = 6 × (1 l) = about 6 × (1 qt) = about 6 qts. Therefore, Kendra drinks 6 quarts of milk a week. Since Kim drinks 2 gallons of milk a week, and there are 4 quarts in one gallon, she then drinks 2 × 4 quarts, or 8 quarts of milk in one week. Since Kendra drinks only 6 quarts of milk in one week, Kim drinks 2 quarts of milk a week more than Kendra.

For a quick estimate, to change from gallons to liters, replace every one gallon by 4 liters. 2 gal = 2 × (4 l) = about 8 l. Therefore, Kim drinks 8 liters of milk in one week. Since Kendra drinks only 6 liters of milk in one week, Kim drinks 2 liters of milk a week more than Kendra.

31 □ The woman who owned the farm had 10-1/2 gallons of milk in each of her two cans. Since 10 gal = 2 × (5 gal) = about 2 × (19 l) = about 38 l, and 1/2 gal = 2 qts = about 2 l, the woman, therefore, had 40 liters of milk in each of her two cans, which we will call can A and can B. Now:

1) Fill Kurt's 5-liter can with milk from can A.

2) Pour the milk from the 5-liter can into the 4-liter can. There will be one liter of milk left in the 5-liter can.
3) Empty the milk in Erick's 4-liter can into can A.
4) Pour the milk in the 5-liter can into the 4-liter can.
5) Fill the 5-liter can with milk from can A.
6) Fill the 4-liter can with milk from the 5-liter can. There will now be 2 liters of milk left in Kurt's 5-liter can.
7) Empty the milk in the 4-liter can into can A.
8) Fill the 4-liter can with milk from can B.
9) Pour the milk from the 4-liter can into can A. This will fill can A. There are now 2 liters of milk left in Erick's 4-liter can.

32 □ If your answer was 10.6 centimeters, then you fell into a trap. When the two cookbooks are side by side on the shelf, the first page of the first cookbook and the last page of the second cookbook are separated only by two covers, the front cover of the first cookbook and the back cover of the second cookbook. Therefore, the bookworm only ate its way through those two covers. Each cover of each book is 3 mm thick, and 3 mm + 3 mm = 6 mm. To change 6 millimeters to centimeters, you replace the millimeters by something that means the same thing in centimeters. Thus, 6 mm = 6 × (1 mm) = 6 × (0.1 cm) = 0.6 cm. Therefore, the total distance that the bookworm traveled was 0.6 centimeters.

33 □ Kendra takes a 250 milligram tablet of Vitamin C each day from Halloween through April Fools' Day, inclusive. Therefore she takes her first 250 milligram tablet on October 31, and she takes her last 250 milligram tablet on April 1. She also takes one 250 milligram tablet on every day that comes between October 31 and April 1. Thus, Kendra takes one 250 mg tablet

on October 31, 30 of them in November, 31 in December, 31 in January, 29 in February (because it is a leap year), 31 in March, and 1 on April 1st. $1 + 30 + 31 + 31 + 29 + 31 + 1 = 154$. This accounts for 154×250 mg = 38,500 mg of Vitamin C. Kendra also takes one 100 milligram tablet of Vitamin C a day on all of the other days of the leap year, of which there are $366 - 154 = 212$. This accounts for 212×100 mg = 21,200 mg of Vitamin C. Therefore, 38,500 mg + 21,200 mg = 59,700 mg of Vitamin C. To change 59,700 milligrams to grams, you replace the milligrams by something that means the same thing in grams. Thus, 59,700 mg = $59,700 \times (1$ mg$)$ = $59,700 \times (0.001$ g$)$ = 59.7 g. Therefore, in one leap year, Kendra takes 59.7 grams of orange-flavored Vitamin C.

34 □ In order to find out how much money Kim brought to the store, you must first find out how many pennies altogether weigh 3 hectograms. First, you must change from 3 hectograms to grams, by replacing the hectograms by something that means the same thing in grams. 3 hg = $3 \times (1$ hg$)$ = $3 \times (100$ g$)$ = 300 g. Now we know that all of Kim's pennies altogether weigh 300 grams. We also know that one penny weighs 3 grams. Therefore, to find out how many pennies weigh 300 grams, you divide by 3 grams. 300 g ÷ 3 g = 100. So Kim's bank contained 100¢ = $1. Thus, we know that Kim brought one dollar's worth of pennies to the store. You use the same method in order to learn the cost of each of Kim's purchases. Kim bought the velvet ribbons for 15 decagrams of pennies. And 15 dkg = $15 \times (1$ dkg$)$ = $15 \times (10$ g$)$ = 150 g. Since 150 g ÷ 3 g = 50, the ribbons must have cost 50¢. She spent 75 grams of pennies to buy the colored pencils. Since 75 g ÷ 3 g = 25, the pencils must have cost 25¢. The crossword-puzzle magazine was purchased for 6 decagrams of pennies. 6 dkg = $6 \times (1$ dkg$)$ = $6 \times (10$ g$)$ = 60

g. Since 69 g ÷ 3 g = 20, the magazine must have cost 20¢. And lastly, the pack of sugarless gum cost 15 g of pennies. Since 15 g ÷ 3 g = 5, the gum must have cost 5¢. Finally, 50¢ + 25¢ + 20¢ + 5¢ = 100¢ = $1.

35 □ We know that the baby bottle from which the baby mountain lion is drinking holds 120 milliliters of milk. We also know that she drinks milk from the same size bottle three times a day. Therefore the baby mountain lion drinks 3 × (120 ml) = 360 ml of milk in one day. Since there are 7 days in one week, she drinks 7 × 360 ml = 2520 ml of milk in one week. In order to find out how many liters of milk she drinks in one week, you must now change 2520 milliliters to liters by replacing the milliliters with something that means the same thing in liters. That is, 2520 ml = 2520 × (1 ml) = 2520 × (0.001 l) = 2.52 l. Thus, the baby mountain lion drinks 2.52 liters of milk in one week.

36 □ The dimensions of the common United States postage stamp are 2 cm by 2-1/2 cm. Therefore, its area is equal to 2 cm × 2-1/2 cm = 5 square centimeters (sq cm).

37 □ The length of Tenney's bed is 30 centimeters. In order for her quilt to touch the floor at both the head of her bed and at the foot of her bed, you must add to the length of the bed the distance that it is from the head of her bed to the floor *and* the distance that it is from the foot of her bed to the floor. Since Tenney's bed is 10 centimeters high, you will therefore add, to the length of her bed, 10 centimeters at the head and 10 centimeters at the foot. That is, 30 cm + 10 cm + 10 cm = 50 cm = the length of Tenney's quilt. Similarly, in order for Tenney's quilt to touch the floor on both sides of her bed, you must add to the width of her bed the distance that it is from each of the two

sides of her bed to the floor. Thus, the width of Tenney's quilt is 20 cm + 10 cm + 10 cm = 40 cm. Now we know that Tenney's quilt is 50 centimeters long and 40 centimeters wide. To find the area of her quilt, in square meters, you must first change from centimeters to meters, by replacing the centimeters by something that means the same thing in meters. That is, 50 cm = 50 × (1 cm) = 50 × (.01 m) = .5 m = the length of Tenney's quilt; 40 cm = (1 cm) = 40 × (.01 m) = .4 m = the width of Tenney's quilt. Therefore, the area of Tenney's quilt is .5 m × .4 m = .2 sq m.

38 □ The volume of a one-quarter pound bar of margarine is equal to its length × its width × its height. Therefore, 12 cm × 3 cm × 3 cm = 108 cubic centimeters (cc) = the volume of a one-quarter pound bar of margarine.

39 □ One liter = 1000 cc, and 1 tablespoon = 15 cc. Therefore, since 1000 cc ÷ 15 cc = 66-2/3, 66 omelets can be made.

40 □ In order to decide whether or not Erick will be able to go sledding today, convert 30°C to degrees Fahrenheit: 9/5 × 30° = 54°, and 54° + 32° = 86°. Therefore, 30°C is the same as 86°F, and due to the extreme heat, it would be impossible for there to be any snow on the ground, and so Erick could not go sledding. Another way to decide, without converting to degrees Fahrenheit, is to note that the temperature at which water freezes is the same as the temperature at which snow melts. At sea level the temperature at which water freezes and snow melts is 0°C, and 30°C is thirty Celsius degrees warmer than that.

41 □ The weight of the head is equal to 250 g (the weight of the

tail) plus one half the weight of the body. By doubling each weight mentioned in this statement, we find that double the weight of the head equals 500 g plus the weight of the body. Since the weight of the body equals the weight of the head plus 250 g (the weight of the tail), we see that double the weight of the head equals 500 g plus the weight of the head plus 250 g. Then the weight of the head must be 750 g.

Since the weight of the body of Kim's fish is equal to the weight of the head + the weight of the tail, the body of the fish weighs 750 g + 250 g = 1000 g. Therefore, the whole fish weighs 750 g + 250 g + 1000 g = 2000 g. In order to find out how many kilograms Kim's fish weighs, you must now change 2000 grams to kilograms, by replacing the grams with something that means the same thing in kilograms. That is, 2000 g = 2 × (1000 g) = 2 × (1 kg) = 2 kg = the weight of Kim's fish.

42 □ The air plant will weigh 1/2 kilogram after 19-1/2 minutes. Since 1 kilogram = 1000 grams, 500 grams is the same as 1/2 kilogram, and thus the air plant will weigh 500 grams after the same 19-1/2 minutes.

43 □ The speed at which the bus traveled is 3 times as fast as the rate at which Kurt and Erick walked. Therefore their walking time was 3 times as great as their riding time. Then their riding time was 1/4 of the total trip time of 8 hours. One-fourth of 8 hours is 2 hours. Therefore, the bus trip from Branford to Sleeping Giant Park took 2 hours. 60 km per hour × 2 hours = 120 km. Therefore, Sleeping Giant Park is 120 kilometers from Branford.

44 □ If Crosswood has 45 miles of streets, then 9 snowplows clear an average of 5 miles of street apiece. And 5 miles =

about 8 km. Thus, each snowplow, on the average, clears 8 kilometers of streets.

45 □ When Walden made his first trip, he traveled faster than the bicycle that he had just left. Therefore, he reached the second bicycle first. This gave him time to fly back to the first bicycle. When Walden flew back to the first bicycle, he again got there first, and thus, he had time for yet another trip. In fact, after every trip that Walden made, he had time for another trip. Therefore, Walden made an infinite number of trips. And yet, although he made an infinite number of trips, he did, in fact, travel a definite distance. The two bicyclists closed the 400 kilometer gap between them at a speed of 40 kilometers per hour. Therefore the two bicyclists met, and crashed, in 10 hours. In that time, Walden flew 32 km per hour × 10 hours, or 320 km.

46 □ Since one teaspoon = 5 cubic centimeters, then 2 tsp. = 2 × (5 cc) = 10 cc. Therefore, Erick sprinkled more sugar on his cereal than Kurt. And, since 10 ml = 10 cc, Kim sprinkled the same amount of sugar onto her cereal as Erick did on his. And since we already know that Erick used more sugar than Kurt, then so did Kim. Thus, the answer is both Erick *and* Kim.

47 □ The unit could not be the pound, because 3 pounds is not a normal birth-weight for a full-term baby. However, since 10 kg = 22 lbs, 3 kg = 6.6 lbs, which is in the normal range of birth-weights. Therefore, the missing unit is likely to be kilograms.

48 □ 50 hectares = 50 × (1 hectare) = 50 × (10,000 square meters) = 500,000 square meters is the area of Peddler's Drive Farm.

49 □ 1 cm = 10 mm. Therefore 1/2 cm = 5 mm.

50 □ Since 10 meters = about 11 yards, 30 meters = about 33 yards. Therefore, 30 meters is longer than 32 yards.

51 □ milli = one-thousandth of   deca = ten times
      centi = one-hundredth of   kilo = one thousand times

52 □ The gap between them grew at the rate of 10 meters per minute. They were next together when the gap had grown to a full lap, or the length of the track. One hour and 20 minutes = 80 min. In that time, the gap between them grew to be 80 × 10 m = 80 × (11 yds) = 880 yds = 2640 ft = 1/2 mile. So the track is a half mile long.

THE ORIGIN OF
THE METRIC SYSTEM

The metric system was first introduced by the French government in 1791. It was designed to accomplish two purposes: 1) to provide natural units of measurement that would make sense for people anywhere on the Earth; 2) to simplify the arithmetic needed for changing from one unit to a larger or smaller unit.

To achieve the first purpose, the units of length and weight were based on the Earth and water respectively. The standard unit of length, called the meter, was obtained in this way: a circle drawn on the surface of the Earth through the North Pole and the South Pole is called a *meridian.* One-fourth of a meridian is called a *quadrant.* It is the distance on a meridian from the North Pole to the Equator. The *meter* was chosen to be one ten-millionth of a quadrant. That is, if a quadrant of a meridian is divided into ten million equal parts, each of these parts is a meter long. Careful measurements were made on the surface of the Earth to find out what the length of a meter is. Then two lines separated by this length were scratched on a platinum bar to serve as a standard against which all meter rods could be checked. This platinum bar is kept in a vault in Paris.

The standard unit of weight was obtained in this way: if a meter is divided into a hundred equal parts, each part is a *centimeter.* A cube whose length, width, and height are all one centimeter long has a volume that is called a cubic centimeter.

A volume of 1000 cubic centimeters is called a liter. The unit of weight was chosen to be the weight of a liter of water at certain standard conditions of temperature and pressure, and it was called a *kilogram*. Since there are 1000 grams in a kilogram, and there are 1000 cubic centimeters in a liter, a *gram* is the weight of one cubic centimeter of water.

To achieve the second purpose, the number ten was chosen as the basis of all groupings of smaller units to form larger units. This choice makes the grouping of units in the metric system match the grouping by tens that underlies our way of writing numbers in the Arabic system of numerals. Then, as we saw on page 26, changing from one unit to another in the metric system can be accomplished by merely moving the decimal point.

In 1960 the meter was redefined in terms of another length found in nature, the wavelength of a certain reddish-orange light sent out by excited atoms of the chemical element krypton 86. A meter is now defined as 1,650,763.73 times this wavelength!

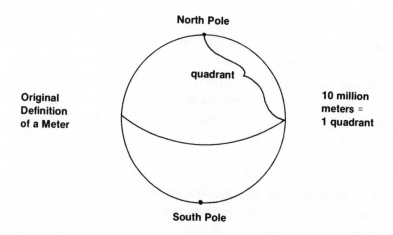

North Pole

quadrant

**Original
Definition
of a Meter**

**10 million
meters =
1 quadrant**

South Pole

metricmetric

CONVERSION TABLES FOR LENGTHS

Inches to Centimeters

1 in	=	2.54 cm
2 in	=	5.08 cm
3 in	=	7.62 cm
4 in	=	10.16 cm
5 in	=	12.70 cm
6 in	=	15.24 cm
7 in	=	17.78 cm
8 in	=	20.32 cm
9 in	=	22.86 cm

10 in	=	25.40 cm
20 in	=	50.80 cm
30 in	=	76.20 cm
40 in	=	101.60 cm
50 in	=	127.00 cm
60 in	=	152.40 cm
70 in	=	177.80 cm
80 in	=	203.20 cm
90 in	=	228.60 cm

100 in	=	254.00 cm

Centimeters to Inches

1 cm	=	0.39 in
2 cm	=	0.79 in
3 cm	=	1.18 in
4 cm	=	1.57 in
5 cm	=	1.97 in
6 cm	=	2.36 in
7 cm	=	2.76 in
8 cm	=	3.15 in
9 cm	=	3.54 in

10 cm	=	3.94 in
20 cm	=	7.87 in
30 cm	=	11.81 in
40 cm	=	15.75 in
50 cm	=	19.69 in
60 cm	=	23.62 in
70 cm	=	27.56 in
80 cm	=	31.50 in
90 cm	=	35.43 in

100 cm	=	39.37 in

metricmetric

CONVERSION TABLES FOR LENGTHS

Yards to Meters

1 yd	=	0.91 m
2 yd	=	1.83 m
3 yd	=	2.74 m
4 yd	=	3.66 m
5 yd	=	4.57 m
6 yd	=	5.49 m
7 yd	=	6.40 m
8 yd	=	7.32 m
9 yd	=	8.23 m

10 yd	=	9.14 m
20 yd	=	18.29 m
30 yd	=	27.43 m
40 yd	=	36.58 m
50 yd	=	45.72 m
60 yd	=	54.86 m
70 yd	=	64.01 m
80 yd	=	73.15 m
90 yd	=	82.30 m

100 yd	=	91.44 m

Meters to Yards

1 m	=	1.09 yd
2 m	=	2.19 yd
3 m	=	3.28 yd
4 m	=	4.37 yd
5 m	=	5.47 yd
6 m	=	6.56 yd
7 m	=	7.66 yd
8 m	=	8.75 yd
9 m	=	9.84 yd

10 m	=	10.94 yd
20 m	=	21.87 yd
30 m	=	32.81 yd
40 m	=	43.74 yd
50 m	=	54.68 yd
60 m	=	65.62 yd
70 m	=	76.55 yd
80 m	=	87.49 yd
90 m	=	98.42 yd

100 m	=	109.36 yd

metricmetric

CONVERSION TABLES FOR DISTANCE

Miles to Kilometers

1 mi	=	1.61 km
2 mi	=	3.22 km
3 mi	=	4.83 km
4 mi	=	6.44 km
5 mi	=	8.05 km
6 mi	=	9.66 km
7 mi	=	11.26 km
8 mi	=	12.87 km
9 mi	=	14.48 km
10 mi	=	16.09 km
20 mi	=	32.19 km
30 mi	=	48.28 km
40 mi	=	64.37 km
50 mi	=	80.46 km
60 mi	=	96.56 km
70 mi	=	112.65 km
80 mi	=	128.74 km
90 mi	=	144.83 km
100 mi	=	160.93 km

Kilometers to Miles

1 km	=	0.62 mi
2 km	=	1.24 mi
3 km	=	1.86 mi
4 km	=	2.49 mi
5 km	=	3.11 mi
6 km	=	3.73 mi
7 km	=	4.35 mi
8 km	=	4.97 mi
9 km	=	5.59 mi
10 km	=	6.21 mi
20 km	=	12.43 mi
30 km	=	18.64 mi
40 km	=	24.86 mi
50 km	=	31.07 mi
60 km	=	37.28 mi
70 km	=	43.50 mi
80 km	=	49.71 mi
90 km	=	55.93 mi
100 km	=	62.14 mi

metricmetric

metricmetric

CONVERSION TABLES FOR AREA

Square Yards to Square Meters

1 sq yd	=	0.84	sq m
2 sq yd	=	1.67	sq m
3 sq yd	=	2.51	sq m
4 sq yd	=	3.34	sq m
5 sq yd	=	4.18	sq m
6 sq yd	=	5.02	sq m
7 sq yd	=	5.85	sq m
8 sq yd	=	6.69	sq m
9 sq yd	=	7.53	sq m
10 sq yd	=	8.36	sq m
20 sq yd	=	16.72	sq m
30 sq yd	=	25.08	sq m
40 sq yd	=	33.45	sq m
50 sq yd	=	41.81	sq m
60 sq yd	=	50.17	sq m
70 sq yd	=	58.53	sq m
80 sq yd	=	66.89	sq m
90 sq yd	=	75.25	sq m
100 sq yd	=	83.61	sq m

Square Meters to Square Yards

1 sq m	=	1.20	sq yd
2 sq m	=	2.39	sq yd
3 sq m	=	3.59	sq yd
4 sq m	=	4.78	sq yd
5 sq m	=	5.98	sq yd
6 sq m	=	7.18	sq yd
7 sq m	=	8.37	sq yd
8 sq m	=	9.57	sq yd
9 sq m	=	10.76	sq yd
10 sq m	=	11.96	sq yd
20 sq m	=	23.92	sq yd
30 sq m	=	35.88	sq yd
40 sq m	=	47.84	sq yd
50 sq m	=	59.80	sq yd
60 sq m	=	71.76	sq yd
70 sq m	=	83.72	sq yd
80 sq m	=	95.68	sq yd
90 sq m	=	107.64	sq yd
100 sq m	=	119.60	sq yd

metricmetric

CONVERSION TABLES FOR VOLUME

Cubic Inches to
Cubic Centimeters

1 cu in	=	16.39 cc
2 cu in	=	32.77 cc
3 cu in	=	49.16 cc
4 cu in	=	65.55 cc
5 cu in	=	81.94 cc
6 cu in	=	98.32 cc
7 cu in	=	114.71 cc
8 cu in	=	131.10 cc
9 cu in	=	147.48 cc

10 cu in	=	163.87 cc
20 cu in	=	327.74 cc
30 cu in	=	491.61 cc
40 cu in	=	655.49 cc
50 cu in	=	819.36 cc
60 cu in	=	983.23 cc
70 cu in	=	1147.10 cc
80 cu in	=	1310.97 cc
90 cu in	=	1474.84 cc

100 cu in	=	1638.72 cc

Cubic Centimeters to
Cubic Inches

1 cc	=	0.06 cu in
2 cc	=	0.12 cu in
3 cc	=	0.18 cu in
4 cc	=	0.24 cu in
5 cc	=	0.31 cu in
6 cc	=	0.37 cu in
7 cc	=	0.43 cu in
8 cc	=	0.49 cu in
9 cc	=	0.55 cu in

10 cc	=	0.61 cu in
20 cc	=	1.22 cu in
30 cc	=	1.83 cu in
40 cc	=	2.44 cu in
50 cc	=	3.05 cu in
60 cc	=	3.66 cu in
70 cc	=	4.27 cu in
80 cc	=	4.88 cu in
90 cc	=	5.49 cu in

100 cc	=	6.10 cu in

metricmetric

metricmetric

Liquid Quarts to Liters				Liters to Liquid Quarts		
1 qt	=	0.95 l		1 l	=	1.06 qt
2 qt	=	1.89 l		2 l	=	2.11 qt
3 qt	=	2.84 l		3 l	=	3.17 qt
4 qt	=	3.79 l		4 l	=	4.23 qt
5 qt	=	4.73 l		5 l	=	5.28 qt
6 qt	=	5.68 l		6 l	=	6.34 qt
7 qt	=	6.62 l		7 l	=	7.40 qt
8 qt	=	7.57 l		8 l	=	8.45 qt
9 qt	=	8.52 l		9 l	=	9.51 qt
10 qt	=	9.46 l		10 l	=	10.57 qt
20 qt	=	18.93 l		20 l	=	21.13 qt
30 qt	=	28.39 l		30 l	=	31.70 qt
40 qt	=	37.85 l		40 l	=	42.27 qt
50 qt	=	47.32 l		50 l	=	52.84 qt
60 qt	=	56.78 l		60 l	=	63.40 qt
70 qt	=	66.24 l		70 l	=	73.97 qt
80 qt	=	75.71 l		80 l	=	84.54 qt
90 qt	=	85.17 l		90 l	=	95.10 qt
100 qt	=	94.63 l		100 l	=	105.67 qt

metricmetric

CONVERSION TABLES FOR WEIGHT

Ounces to Grams				Grams to Ounces		
1 oz	=	28.35 g		1 g	=	0.04 oz
2 oz	=	56.70 g		2 g	=	0.07 oz
3 oz	=	85.05 g		3 g	=	0.11 oz
4 oz	=	113.40 g		4 g	=	0.14 oz
5 oz	=	141.75 g		5 g	=	0.18 oz
6 oz	=	170.10 g		6 g	=	0.21 oz
7 oz	=	198.45 g		7 g	=	0.25 oz
8 oz	=	226.80 g		8 g	=	0.28 oz
9 oz	=	255.15 g		9 g	=	0.32 oz
10 oz	=	283.50 g		10 g	=	0.35 oz
20 oz	=	567.00 g		20 g	=	0.71 oz
30 oz	=	850.49 g		30 g	=	1.06 oz
40 oz	=	1133.99 g		40 g	=	1.41 oz
50 oz	=	1417.49 g		50 g	=	1.77 oz
60 oz	=	1700.99 g		60 g	=	2.12 oz
70 oz	=	1984.49 g		70 g	=	2.47 oz
80 oz	=	2267.99 g		80 g	=	2.82 oz
90 oz	=	2551.48 g		90 g	=	3.18 oz
100 oz	=	2834.98 g		100 g	=	3.53 oz

metricmetric

Pounds to Kilograms

1 lb	=	0.45 kg
2 lb	=	0.91 kg
3 lb	=	1.36 kg
4 lb	=	1.81 kg
5 lb	=	2.27 kg
6 lb	=	2.72 kg
7 lb	=	3.18 kg
8 lb	=	3.63 kg
9 lb	=	4.08 kg
10 lb	=	4.54 kg
20 lb	=	9.07 kg
30 lb	=	13.61 kg
40 lb	=	18.14 kg
50 lb	=	22.68 kg
60 lb	=	27.22 kg
70 lb	=	31.75 kg
80 lb	=	36.29 kg
90 lb	=	40.82 kg
100 lb	=	45.36 kg

Kilograms to Pounds

1 kg	=	2.20 lb
2 kg	=	4.41 lb
3 kg	=	6.61 lb
4 kg	=	8.82 lb
5 kg	=	11.02 lb
6 kg	=	13.23 lb
7 kg	=	15.43 lb
8 kg	=	17.64 lb
9 kg	=	19.84 lb
10 kg	=	22.05 lb
20 kg	=	44.09 lb
30 kg	=	66.14 lb
40 kg	=	88.18 lb
50 kg	=	110.23 lb
60 kg	=	132.28 lb
70 kg	=	154.32 lb
80 kg	=	176.37 lb
90 kg	=	198.41 lb
100 kg	=	220.46 lb

metricmetric